The Trial of Viscountess Belmore, (Formerly Lady Henrietta Hobart, and Daughter to John Earl of Buckinghamshire) for Adultery with The Earl of Ancram, including The Depositions of The Earl on Enniskillen, Sir R. Heron, and all the Other Witnesses

Anonymous

The Trial of Viscountess Belmore, (Formerly Lady Henrietta Hobart, and Daughter to John Earl of Buckinghamshire) for Adultery with The Earl of Ancram, including The Depositions of The Earl on Enniskillen, Sir R. Heron, and all the Other Witnesses

Trial of Henrietta Belmore - 1793
NYB02226
Monograph
New York City Bar
London: Printed for T. Salisbury; and Sold at No 293, Oxford-Road, and under the Piazza, Covent-Garden; and all the Booksellers in Town and Country. 1793

The Making of Modern Law collection of legal archives constitutes a genuine revolution in historical legal research because it opens up a wealth of rare and previously inaccessible sources in legal, constitutional, administrative, political, cultural, intellectual, and social history. This unique collection consists of three extensive archives that provide insight into more than 300 years of American and British history. These collections include:

Legal Treatises, 1800-1926: over 20,000 legal treatises provide a comprehensive collection in legal history, business and economics, politics and government.

Trials, 1600-1926: nearly 10,000 titles reveal the drama of famous, infamous, and obscure courtroom cases in America and the British Empire across three centuries.

Primary Sources, 1620-1926: includes reports, statutes and regulations in American history, including early state codes, municipal ordinances, constitutional conventions and compilations, and law dictionaries.

These archives provide a unique research tool for tracking the development of our modern legal system and how it has affected our culture, government, business – nearly every aspect of our everyday life. For the first time, these high-quality digital scans of original works are available via print-on-demand, making them readily accessible to libraries, students, independent scholars, and readers of all ages.

The BiblioLife Network

This project was made possible in part by the BiblioLife Network (BLN), a project aimed at addressing some of the huge challenges facing book preservationists around the world. The BLN includes libraries, library networks, archives, subject matter experts, online communities and library service providers. We believe every book ever published should be available as a high-quality print reproduction; printed on-demand anywhere in the world. This insures the ongoing accessibility of the content and helps generate sustainable revenue for the libraries and organizations that work to preserve these important materials.

The following book is in the "public domain" and represents an authentic reproduction of the text as printed by the original publisher. While we have attempted to accurately maintain the integrity of the original work, there are sometimes problems with the original work or the micro-film from which the books were digitized. This can result in minor errors in reproduction. Possible imperfections include missing and blurred pages, poor pictures, markings and other reproduction issues beyond our control. Because this work is culturally important, we have made it available as part of our commitment to protecting, preserving, and promoting the world's literature.

GUIDE TO FOLD-OUTS MAPS and OVERSIZED IMAGES

The book you are reading was digitized from microfilm captured over the past thirty to forty years. Years after the creation of the original microfilm, the book was converted to digital files and made available in an online database.

In an online database, page images do not need to conform to the size restrictions found in a printed book. When converting these images back into a printed bound book, the page sizes are standardized in ways that maintain the detail of the original. For large images, such as fold-out maps, the original page image is split into two or more pages

Guidelines used to determine how to split the page image follows:

• Some images are split vertically; large images require vertical and horizontal splits.
• For horizontal splits, the content is split left to right.
• For vertical splits, the content is split from top to bottom.
• For both vertical and horizontal splits, the image is processed from top left to bottom right.

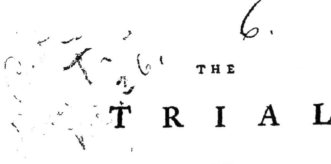

6.

THE

TRIAL

OF

VISCOUNTESS BELMORE,

(FORMERLY LADY HENRIETTA HOBART, AND DAUGHTER
TO JOHN EARL OF BUCKINGHAMSHIRE)

FOR

ADULTERY

WITH THE

EARL OF ANCRAM,

INCLUDING

THE DEPOSITIONS OF THE EARL OF ENNISKILLEN, SIR
F. HERON, AND ALL THE OTHER WITNESSES.

LONDON:

PRINTED FOR T. SALISBURY;

And Sold at N° 293, Oxford-Road, and under the Piazza
Covent-Garden and all the Bookfellers in Town and
Country

1793

COPY OF DEPOSITIONS.

May 4, 1792.

The Reverend JOHN LOWRY of Somerfet, in the county of Tyrone, in the kingdom of Ireland, aged forty-two years and upwards, a witnefs produced and fworn.

TO the fecond and third articles of the faid libel, this deponent fays, he is now and hath been for upwards of twenty years laft paft, intimately acquainted with the right honourable Armar Lowry Corry, Vifcount Belmore, of the kingdom of Ireland, (formerly Armar Lowry Corry, Efq) the party in this caufe , and he further fays, that he has now, and hath had for about eighteen years, a benefice in the See of Armagh, in the faid kingdom of Ireland, and it is not cuftomary in his parifh, and he believes in no other parifh within the faid kingdom, for any regifter to be made of mar-

B

riages

...ages solemnized within the said Kingdom. And
this deponent further says, that during his acquaintance with the said Lord Belmore, he frequently visited him, since about eleven years since,
as he now best recollects as to time, and within
-bout six months after the marriage of the said
Lord Belmore, then Armar Lowry Corry, Esq.
with the articulate right honourable lady Henrietta Hobart, now Viscountess Belmore, this deponent and his wife went to the said Lord Belmore's (then Armar Lowry Corry) seat, at Castle
Coole, in the county of Fermanagh, in the said
Kingdom of Ireland, for the purpose of paying
his respects to him on his late marriage, and
this deponent and his said wife continued on such
visit at Castle Coole for a week, and some time
afterwards this deponent was again on a visit at
Castle Coole, for two or three days, and during
said two visits at Castle Coole aforesaid, they the
said Armar Lowry Corry, afterwards Viscount
Belmore, and they the said right honourable lady
Henrietta Hobart, afterwards Belmore, his wife,
lived and cohabited together at Castle Coole
aforesaid, as lawful husband and wife, and constantly owned and acknowledged each other as
such, and were and are so universally esteemed
and taken to be by their relations, friends, ac-
quaintances, and others, and further to the said
articles or either of them he cannot depose save
that he always understood, that the said Lord Belmore

more was married at the Castle in Dublin, within
the said kingdom of Ireland, and also he that
within or about a year that the said marriage, the
said Lady Belmore was delivered of a daughter,
which is still living.

To the fourth article of the libel and that the
deponent says, that when he to visited Castle
Coole, as before set forth, soon after the aforesaid marriage, he the said right honourable
Armar Lowry Corry, Viscount Belmore, then
Lord Belmore, behaved to his wife, the said
right honourable Lady Henrietta, Viscountess
Corry, now Belmore, with the greatest love and
attention, and appeared to do every thing possible to win and to retain her affection, but appa-
rently without success, for the said right
honourable Lady Henrietta Corry, now Viscountess Belmore, at all times when this deponent was present, behaved in such a manner towards the said right honourable Lord Lowry
Corry, now Viscount Belmore, as to convince this
deponent and the others present, by his whole
his behaviour, that she had no love for him, and
the said Viscount Belmore. And this deponent
further says, that not—— of the love for
Belmore, then said Belmore, for the only one
daughter, and be left living, his wife the Viscount, then Lord Belmore, and was said Lord
Viscountess, then Lady Belmore, deponent doth

each other, and this deponent believes the said Viscount Belmore hath not once lived or cohabited with his said wife ; and further to this article he cannot depose.

To the thirteenth article of the said allegation, this deponent says, that during the last eleven months, he hath repeatedly seen the aforesaid right honourable Armar Lowry Corry, Viscount Belmore, at his seat called Castle Coole, and in other places, in the said kingdom of Ireland , and this deponent doth verily believe, and is well convinced, that the said Viscount Belmore, during the said period of eleven months, hath not been out of the said kingdom of Ireland, or had any intercourse or connection with the said right honourable Henrietta, Viscountess Belmore, his wife: and further he cannot depose.

JOHN LOWRY.

CHARLES

MAY 4, 1792.

CHARLES KING, of Rutland-square, East, in the county of Dublin, in the kingdom of Ireland, Esq aged fifty-two years and upwards, a witness produced and sworn.

TO the second article of the said libel, this deponent says, he is now and hath been for upwards of twenty years last past, law-agent to the right honourable Armar Lowry Corry, Viscount Belmore, of the kingdom of Ireland, (formerly Armar Lowry Corry, Esq.) one of the parties in this cause, who on or about the 12th day of March, 1780, (as this deponent best recollects) intermarried with the right honourable Lady Henrietta Hobart, now Viscountess Belmore, the other party in this cause. That this deponent dined with him on the day the day the marriage took place, and he believes they were married in the castle, (being the residence of the Lord Lieutenant) in the parish of St. Werburgh, within the said city of Dublin. And this deponent further saith, that within the last two months, he hath made diligent search in the registry belonging to the said parish of St. Werburgh, and hath not been able to find any entry of the aforesaid marriage, and he believes there was not any entry made thereof in the books belonging to the said parish; and this deponent further says, he hath made enquiries of those most likely to give

give him information, and he hath heard and believes, that it is not usual or customary for any register to be made of marriages had and solemnized in the Castle, of the said city of Dublin, and further to the said article he cannot depose.

To the third article of the said libel this deponent says, that soon after the solemnization of the said marriage, they the said Armar Lowry Corry, now Viscount Belmore, and the said Henrietta Corry, formerly Hobart, his wife, went to live and reside at the houses of the said Armar Lowry Corry, Viscount Belmore, at Castle Coole, in the county of Fermanagh, and at Dublin, within the said kingdom of Ireland, and there consummated their said marriage, and in about thirteen or fourteen months after the said marriage, she the said Henrietta Corry, formerly Hobart, now Viscountess Belmore, was delivered of a daughter, who is now living; and they the said Armar Lowry Corry, afterwards Viscount Belmore, and the said Lady Henrietta Corry, afterwards Belmore, his wife, did continue so to live and cohabit together, as husband and wife, until about a month or six weeks after the birth of the said child, when they entered into articles of separation, and a separation took place between them accordingly. And this deponent further saith, that from and after the solemnization of the aforesaid marriage, they the said Armar Lowry Corry, now Viscount Belmore, and

and the said Henrietta Corry, formerly Hobart, now also Belmore his wife constantly, and upon all occasions loved and acknowledged each other as being husband and wife, and [...] and [...] for [...] establishments, and taken to be by their relations, friends, acquaintance and others, and further to the said article he cannot depose.

To the fourth article of the said libel, this deponent says, that from the time of the solemnization of the aforesaid marriage until the separation took place, as before set forth, he was frequently in company with the parties in this cause, and he can take upon himself to say positively, he was in company with them, during the said period, upwards of twenty times, and he the said Armar Lowry Corry, now Viscount Belmore, whenever this deponent was present, behaved to his said wife, the said Henrietta Corry, formerly Hobart, now Viscountess Belmore, with the greatest love and affection, and appeared to be, and was, as this deponent doth verily believe, desirous of doing every thing in his power to to please her, and the said Henrietta Corry, formerly Hobart, now Viscountess Belmore, at all times when this deponent was present, conducted herself towards the said Armar Lowry Corry, now Viscount Belmore, in such a manner, as convinced this deponent, and he believes every person who saw her conduct, that she had not any

regard

regard or affection whatever for the said Armar Lowry Corry, now Viscount Belmore, who declared to this deponent, that it was not possible for them to continue to live together. And after the birth of the aforesaid daughter, this deponent received instructions from the said Amar Lowry Corry, then Lord Belmore, and now Viscount Belmore, to prepare articles of separation between him and his aforesaid wife, which being prepared, they executed the same in this deponent's presence, and soon afterwards separated accordingly, about a month or six weeks after the birth of the said child; and this deponent believes they have not since lived or cohabited together; and farther to this article he cannot depose.

To the thirteenth article of the said libel, this deponent says, that in or about the month of June last, the aforesaid right honourable Armar Lowry Corry, Viscount Belmore, returned from England to Ireland, since which this deponent hath had constant intercourse with him every fortnight, either personally, or by letter, and he doth verily and in his conscience believe, and is well convinced, that since the said month of June, the said Armar Lowry Corry, Viscount Belmore, hath not been out of the said kingdom of Ireland, or had any intercourse or connection with the said right honourable Lady Henrietta Viscountess Belmore, his wife; and further he cannot depose.

CHARLES KING.

May 7, 1792.

ARTHUR KEMPLAND, of the Rue de Præ-
tor, in the town of Calais, in the kingdom of
France, Esq. aged forty-seven years and upwards, a witness produced and sworn.

To the sixth, seventh, and eighth articles of
the said libel, this deponent says, he hath known
and been well acquainted with the persons of the
articulate right honourable Henrietta Viscountess
Belmore, party in this cause, formerly the right
honourable Lady Henrietta Hobart, and of the
right honourable William Kerr, commonly called
Earl of Ancram, formerly the right honourable
William Kerr, commonly called Lord Newbattle,
for upwards of fourteen years last past, and some
time in or about the latter end of the month of
September, this deponent being then at Calais
aforesaid, he there at two or three different times,
saw the said right honourable Henrietta Viscountess
Belmore, and the said right honourable William
Kerr, commonly called Earl of Ancram, walking
arm and arm, together, about the streets of
Calais; and this deponent then understood from
a seaman belonging to a vessel then in the har-
bour, that he had brought Lord Ancram, and
the lady that was with him, from Broad Stairs,
and that they had been wind-bound. And this

C   de-

deponent further fays, that in the month of December following, and as he now beft recollects it was on or about the eighth day of the faid month, being in the market-place, in the faid town of Calais, he again faw the aforefaid Lord Ancram and Lady Belmore, and this deponent at fuch time followed them to a pnblic inn in the faid town, fituate in the Rue Royal, commonly known by the name of l'Hotel d'Angleterre, kept by Monfieur Deffein. And this deponent laftly fays, that the lady he fo as aforefaid faw at Calais, was in company with the faid William Kerr, commonly called Earl of Ancram, and the right honourable Henrietta Vifcountefs Belmore, party in this caufe, was, and is one and the fame perfon, and not divers; and further to the faid articles or either of them he cannot depofe.

ARTHUR KEMPLAND.

JANET

JANET HURE, of the Rue de Lion Rouge, in
the town of Calais, in the kingdom of France,
Spinster, aged eighteen years and upwards, a
witness produced and sworn.

TO the seventh, eighth, and ninth articles of
the said libel, this deponent says, that on the
eighth day of December last, Monsieur Dessein,
who keeps the Hotel d'Angleterre, in Calais
aforesaid, came to this deponent, and informed
her, that an English Lord and Lady were at his
house, and that they wanted a chamber-maid,
and asked her if she was inclined to take that
place, that accordingly she went to the house of
the said Monsieur Dessein, and was by him introduced to a lady, who, he informed this deponent, was the wife of an English Lord, who
had been married to her two years; that the said
Lady agreed to take this deponent into her service, in the capacity of chamber-maid, and on
the following day, this deponent, by order of the
said Lady, who went by the name of Lady Ancram, went to a house in a village, called by the
name of Rushleigh, situate about seven miles
from Calais, on the road leading to Boulogne,
which house had, as this deponent understood,
been taken by the said Lord Ancram, of a Ma-
dam Colbere. And this deponent further says,

C 2

that on the eleventh of the said month the said Lord and Lady Ancram came to the said house at Rushleigh; and the family then confisted of Lord and Lady Ancram, two men servants of the name of La Duc and Augustein, the cook named Catherine Baffin, and this deponent. And she further says, that herself and the aforesaid servants, continued to live at the said house with Lord and Lady Ancram for six weeks, during which time this deponent, almost every morning, saw the said Lord Ancram, and the person who was then called Lady Ancram, in one and the same bed together, naked and alone, and from what this deponent hath since learnt, she doth believe, that the person who then went by the name of Lady Ancram, at such time, committed the foul crime of adultery. And this deponent further says, that when she so lived with the said Lord and Lady Ancram, they paffed for husband and wife, and as such were considered by the deponent, and as she believes by those living in the neighbourhood of the said house. And this deponent further says, that when she had as aforesaid lived for about six weeks with the said Lord and Lady Ancram, she was of a sudden ordered by the said Lady Ancram to pack up every thing, as she had received letters from England, and she must immediately go there; and accordingly about seven o'clock the same evening, Lord and Lady Ancram set out for Calais, and on the following morning,

at

at about three o'clock, this deponent and the cook, and two men-fervants, with the baggage, went to Calais, fince which, fhe hath not feen either Lord Ancram or the Lady, who was then called Lady Ancram, on this deponent taking leave, informed her, in cafe of her return to Calais, fhe would take the deponent again into her fervice; and my Lord's valet, Monfieur le Duc, informed her, that his mafter and miftrefs were to pafs through London, in their way to Scotland. And this deponent laftly fays, that from what fhe hath, fince fhe hath been in the fervice of the aforefaid Lady learnt, fhe doth verily believe, that the Lady who fo cohabited with the right honourable William Kerr, then called Lord Ancram, at bed and board, and went by the name of Lady An-cram, at the aforefaid houfe, belonging to the faid Madame Colbere, and the right honourable Henrietta Vifcountefs Belmore, party in this caufe, was and is one and the fame perfon, and not divers; and further to the faid articles, or either of them, fhe cannot depofe.

JANET HURE.

CATHERINE

CATHERINE BASSIN, of the Rue Royale, in the town of Calais, in the kingdom of France, Spinster, aged twenty-four years and upwards, a witness produced and sworn.

TÓ the seventh, eighth and ninth articles of the said libel, this deponent says, that some time in or about the month of December or January last, on a Thursday, Monsieur Dessein, who keeps an inn at Calais aforesaid, known by the name of l'Hotel d'Angleterre, sent for her, and on her arriving at his house, he informed her, that Lord and Lady Ancram, or that an English Lord and his Lady were there, and that they wanted a cook. That this deponent was then introduced to the said Lady, and then informed it was Lady Ancram, and was then hired by her as her cook; and on the following day, by order of the said Lady, she accompanied by her fellow-witness Janet Hure, went to a country-house taken by the said Lord Ancram, of a Madame Colbere, about three leagues from Paris, at a place called Rushleigh, in the road leading to Boulogne; that on the Sunday following, the aforesaid Lord and Lady Ancram came to the said house at Rushleigh; and when their family so arrived, their family consisted of six persons; to wit, themselves, two valets named Auguste and Le Duc, the chambermaid named Janet Hure, and this deponent.

That

That from the time of this deponent's arriving at
said house at Rushleigh, she continued to live in
their service for six weeks, exactly, during which
time she believed the said Lord and Lady Ancram
to be husband and wife, as they lived and cohabited
together as such; and as husband and wife she believes they were considered, by those who lived in
their neighbourhood, as they at such times passed
for husband and wife, and went by the name of
Lord and Lady Ancram.

That during the time they so lived together at
Rushleigh aforesaid, which was six weeks, they the
said parties had but *one bed* made up for them;
and, as this deponant verily believes and is well
convinced, they the whole of the said time slept in
one and the same bed together *naked* and alone.
That one morning happening, as this deponant
well remembers, the last day of the last year (her
fellow-servant Jane Hure being from home) this
deponent for her, went into the chamber, in which
her master and mistress slept, for the purpose of
lighting their fire; and she this deponent then and
there plainly saw the aforesaid Lord Ancram, and
the person who then went by the name of Lady
Ancram, in one and the same bed, perfectly naked
and alone, the bed-cloaths being partly off, and
from what this deponent hath since learnt, she doth
believe, that the Lady who then passed for the wife
of the said Lord Ancram, did, at the time she so

lived

lived and cohabited with him, and was as aforesaid seen in bed with him by this deponent, commit the foul crime of adultry together, such was the nicety of their situation when this deponent saw them in bed together.

That this deponent at several *other* times, hath seen the said Lord and Lady Ancram *kiss* each other ; but at such time *conceiving* them to be man and wife, she did not particularly remark with what ardency they manifested their amorous tokens.

This deponent further says, that on the Thurf-day morning, which happened six weeks after this deponent first went to live in the service of the said Lord and Lady Ancram, she was by her Lady's valet, Monsieur Le Duc, informed, she must get the linen and things together, for that his master and mistress were going to England, to be present at the marriage of Lord Ancram's sister. That at about six o'clock on the said evening, the said Lord and Lady Ancram set out in a Chaise for Calais, and were on the next morning, at about three o'clock, followed by this deponent and the other servants, since which she hath not seen either her aforesaid master or mistress. And further than believing them to be the same persons as mentioned in this cause, she cannot depose.

The X. mark of
CATHERINE BASSIN.

The Right Honourable WILLIAM EARL of ENNISKILLEN, of the kingdom of Ireland, aged fifty years and upwards, a witnefs produced and fworn.

TO the firft article of the faid libel, this deponent fays, he hath known and been well acquainted with the articulate right honourable Armar Lowry Corry, Vifcount Belmore, formerly Armar Lowry Corry, Efq. for upwards of thirty years laft paft, and fome time in or about the month of March, 1780, he was defired to be prefent at a marriage then intended to be folemnized between the faid Lord Belmore, then Armar Lowry Corry, who was at that time a widower, and paying his addreffes to the articulate right honourable Henrietta Hobart, daughter of the right honourable John Earl of Buckinghamfhire, then Lord Lieutenant of the kingdom of Ireland, who at fuch time was a fpinfter and a minor, of the age of 18 years, or thereabouts, and fome time in or about the faid month of March, 1780, he attended in the caftle in the city of Dublin, the refidence of the faid Lord Lieutenant, and in one of the apartments in the caftle of Dublin, he there faw the faid right honourable Lord Belmore, then Armar Lowry Corry, Efq. one of the parties in this caufe, and the faid right honourable Henrietta Vifcountefs Belmore, then

D   Henrietta

Henrietta Hobart, the other party in this caufe, lawfully joined together in holy matrimony, according to the rites and ceremonies of the eftablifhed churches of England and Ireland, by the Reverend Thomas Barnard, Doctor in Divinity, a prieft or minifter in holy orders, and now Bifhop of Kilaloe, who then and there pronounced them to be hufband and wife, in the prefence of the aforefaid right honourable John Earl of Buckinghamfhire, and his lady, and alfo in the prefence of this deponent's wife, Lady Ennifkillen, and others of the family of the Earl of Buckinghamfhire : and further to this article he cannot depofe.

To the fecond article of the faid libel, this deponent favs, that very lately he hath made enquiries at Dublin, of the moft likely to give him information concerning the bufinefs ; and from the information he hath received, he doth believe that it is not ufual or cuftomary for any regifter to be made of marriages had and folemnized in the caftle, in the faid city of Dublin, and he doth believe that no entry was made of the aforefaid marriage between the parties in this caufe : and further to this article he cannot depofe.

To the third article of the faid libel, this deponent fays, that after the faid marriage was folemnized between the parties in this caufe, they the faid Armar Lowry Corry, afterwards Vifcount Belmore,

more, and the said right honourable Lady Henrietta Corry, formerly Hobart, his wife went to live and reside at the houses of the right honourable Armar Lowry Corry, Viscount Belmore, at Dublin and Castle Coole, in the county of Fermanagh, in the kingdom of Ireland, and had issue, by their said marriage, a daughter now living, and continued so to live and reside together for a year, or thereabouts, during which time they owned and acknowledged each other as lawful husband and wife, and were and are so universally esteemed and taken to be by their relations, friends, acquaintance and others: and further to this article he cannot depose.

To the fourth article of the said libel, this deponent says, that during the time the parties in this cause lived and cohabited together, this deponent very frequently saw them (his house in the country being within eight miles of theirs, and in Dublin, the next street but one to theirs) and very soon after their marriage, he observed that they seemed to live unhappy together, and that there was a visible disgust on the part of the said Lady Belmore, formerly Hobart, towards the aforesaid Lord Belmore formerly Armar Lowry Corry, her husband, and in consequence of their unhappiness, they, about a year after they were married, separated by mutual agreement, and as this deponent doth verily believe, they have not lived nor cohabited together

since:

fince: and further to this article he cannot depofe:

To the thirteenth article of the faid libel this deponent fays, that fince the beginning of the month of June laft, he hath frequently feen the aforefaid Lord Belmore in Ireland, and had other intercourfe by letter; and this deponent doth verily, and in his confcience believe, that he the faid Lord Belmore, fince the beginning of the faid month of June, hath not been out of the faid kingdom of Ireland, or had any intercourfe or connexion with the aforefaid right honourable Henrietta, Vifcountefs Belmore, his wife, who hath not as this deponent doth verily believe, during that time, been in the faid kingdom of Ireland; and further he cannot depofe.

ENNISKILLEN.

FRANCIS

FRANCIS LE DUC, at prefent Valet to Lord Beauchamp, of Berkeley-fquare, in the parifh of St. James, Weftminfter, in the county of Middlefex, aged thirty-three years and upwards, a witnefs produced and fworn.

TO the fourth article of the faid libel, this deponent fays, that fome time in or about the latter end of the fummer of the year 1781, the articulate right honourable Henrietta Vifcountefs Belmore being at Paris, in the kingdom of France, hired him as her footman, and from that time until the fecond day of April laft, he hath continued to live in her fervice as footmen and valet. That fo he lived with the faid Lady Belmore, the party in this caufe, for about five years, at Paris aforefaid, after which he removed with her to a houfe in Welbeck-ftreet, London, and during the whole of the time this deponent fo lived with her, the articulate right honourable Armar Lowry Corry, Vifcount Belmore, party in this caufe, did not live or cohabit with the aforefaid Lady Belmore, and further to this article he cannot depofe.

To the fifth and fixth articles of the faid libel, this deponent fays, that about four years fince, he attended the faid Lady Belmore, on a vifit to feveral of her friends in Scotland, and there fhe

became

became acquainted (as he believes) with the articulate William Kerr, commonly called Lord Ancram. That in the summer of the year 1790, the said Lord Ancram came to London, and was very frequent in his visits to Lady Belmore, who then resided in Welbeck-street aforesaid, and there this deponent believes an *adulterous* intercourse and connection took place between the said Lord Ancram and Lady Belmore, and that they now continue to carry on the same. And this deponent further says, that some time in or about the beginning of the month of August last, the said Lady Belmore, attended by a female servant, and this deponent, went from her said house in Welbeck street to Broad Stairs, in the Isle of Thanet, in the county of Kent, to a ready-furnished house, which she hired for three months. That the aforesaid Lord Ancram, on the same day, took ready furnished apartments at a private house in Broad Stairs aforesaid; and during the time the said Lord Ancram and Lady Belmore so lived at Broad Stairs aforesaid, which was for near three months, they were almost constantly together; and he the said Lord Ancram generally slept at the house of the said Lady Belmore, had a bed-room fitted up for him, and his valet continued to reside at his Lordship's ready-furnished apartments. That during the said time, they the said Lord Ancram and Lady Belmore occasionally made excursions to the neighbour-

ing

ing villages, and were abfent from Broad Stairs all night, and at fuch times were unattended. And that fome time in or about the month of October laft, they the faid Lord Ancram and Lady Belmore, attended by the aforefaid female fervant, who was called Mrs. Bell, Lord An- cram's valet, who was called Auguftus, and this deponent, went on an excurfion to Calais, in the kingdom of France, where they continued for about a fortnight; and this deponent believes, that from the time they fo left London as afore- faid, until the time by him now depofed to, an improper intimacy and connexion fubfifted be- tween the aforefaid right honourable William Kerr, commonly called Lord Ancram, and the afore- faid right honourable Henrietta Vifcountefs Bel- more, party in this caufe, and further to thefe articles, or either of them, he cannot depofe.

To the feventh article of the faid libel, this de- ponent fays, that in the beginning of the month of December laft, and as he now beft recollects it was on or about the third or fourth day of the faid month aforefaid, Lady Belmore having entirely quitted Broad Stairs aforefaid, went from her houfe in Welbeck-ftreet aforefaid, attended by her maid- fervant, the aforefaid Mrs. Bell and this deponent, and proceeded to Shooter's Hill on the road to Dover, and there the faid Lady Belmore left her faid fervant, Mrs. Bell, and proceeded on to Do-

ver,

ver, attended only by this deponent; fhe was two miles on the other fide of the faid Shooter's Hill, joined by the aforefaid Lord Ancram, who then got into the chaife with Lady Belmore, and the proceeded to Calais, in the kingdom of France, where they arrived on the 3d day after they fo left London as aforefaid. That on their arrival at Calais as aforefaid, they went to a public inn there, known by the name of l'Hotel d'Angleterre, kept by Monfieur Deffein, where they continued for a week. That on their arrival at Calais, he received orders from Lord Ancram that in cafe any body afked after him, he was to make anfwer that it was Lord and Lady Ancram. And this deponent further fays, that whilft the faid Lord Ancram and Lady Belmore, then paffing for hufband and wife, and going by the name of Lord and Lady Ancram, were fo at l'Hotel d'Anglerre as aforefaid, they occupied two bed-rooms adjoining to each other. And he further fays, the Lady who fo accompanied the faid Lord Ancram as aforefaid, to Calais, and who went by the name of Lady Ancram and lived and cohabited with the faid William Kerr, commonly called Earl of Ancram at the aforefaid Hotel, as his wife as aforefaid, and the articulate right honourable Henrietta Vifcountefs Belmore, party in this caufe, was and is one and the fame perfon, and not d'vers, and further to this aiticle he cannot depofe.

To

To the eighth article of the said libel, this deponent says, that having staid a week at the house of the said Monsieur Deffein as aforesaid, the aforesaid Lord Ancram and Lady Belmore, then calling themselves Lord and Lady Ancram, attended by two female servants hired at Calais, and this deponent and the aforesaid Augustus (Lord Ancram's valet, who had since arrived at Calais) went to a ready-furnished house situated about a league and a half from Calais, on the road to Boulogne, which house and the neighbourhood is called La Rocherie, where they the said Lord Ancram and Lady Belmore, then passing for husband and wife, and calling themselves Lord and Lady Ancram, continued to reside for six weeks, and their family consisted of four, or they were only attended by four servants, (to wit) Augustus, the two female servants, and this deponent, and they the said right honourable William Kerr, commonly called Earl of Ancram, and the said right honourable Henrietta Viscountess Belmore, whilst at La Rocherie as aforesaid, went by the names of Lord and Lady Ancram, and passed for man and wife, constantly slept in one and the same bed, and thereby committed the foul crime of adultry, and he further says, that the said Lady who so cohabited with the said right honourable William Kerr, commonly called Earl of Ancram, at bed and board, and went by the name of Lady Ancram, at the house called La Rocherie, which is, as this

E   deponent

deponent believs, the property of the articulate
Madame Colbere, and the said right honourable
Henrietta Viscountess Belmore, party in this cause,
was and is one and the same person, and not divers, and further to this article he cannot depose.

To the ninth article of the said libel, this deponant says, that after they had remained about
six weeks at the said house, called La Rocherie,
he received orders from Lord Ancram at about
twelve o'clock at noon, to pack up every thing,
for he believed they must depart for England that
evening, that he was then going to Calais in
order to know whether they were then to go or
not, and accordingly at about five o'clock that
same afternoon, Lord Ancram returned from
Calais, and a post-carriage arriving at the same
time, they the said Lord Ancram and Lady Belmore, then calling themselves Lord and Lady
Ancram, set out almost immediately in the said
post-carriage for Calais, and were early the following morning joined at Calais by this deponent and his fellow-servants. That the said Lord
Ancram and Lady Belmore, attended by Augustus and this deponent, on said following morning,
went on board a packet and sailed for Dover,
where they arrived about noon the same day;
and further to this article he cannot depose, save
that previous to their sailing from Calais, this deponent

ponent by the orders of Lord Ancram, difcharged the aforefaid two female fervants.

To the tenth article of the faid libel, this deponent fays, that as foon as they arrived at Dover, he received orders from Lord Ancram, that in cafe he was afked who they were, thereby meaning the aforefaid Lord Ancram and Lady Belmore, this deponent was to make anfwer that it was Mr. Anderfon and Mrs. Smith, and by fuch names they travelled towards Scotland, while this deponent continued with them. That this deponent travelled with them as far as Newark, in the road to York, and at the different inns they flept at, there were always two bed-rooms ordered for the faid Lord Ancram and Lady Belmore, then ufing the nams of Mr. Anderfon and Mrs. Smith, and further to this article he cannot depofe, fave that the aforefaid Auguftus, Lord Ancram's valet, was left at Dover, in order to take care of his mafter's horfe.

To the eleventh article of the faid libel, this deponent fays, he arrived at Edinburgh before the aforefaid Lord Ancram and Lady Belmore, and on their arrival in or about the latter end of the month of January laft, they took private lodgings in the faid town of Edinburgh, at which place they went by the aforefaid names of Mr. Anderfon and Mrs. Smith, and had in the faid lodgings a bed-

room

room for each of them; that having remained in
the said lodgings for about a fortnight, they took
a ready-furnished house, about three or four miles
from the said town, and there the said Lord Ancram went by his own name, and this deponent
received orders to call the said Lady Belmore,
MyLady! without adding any other name to her
title, and in the said house they also had two bed-
rooms. That the said Lord Ancram and Lady
Belmore continued at the said house for about a
month or five weeks, and further he cannot
depose, save he believes the aforesaid Lord Ancram
and Lady Belmore, whilst in Scotland as aforesaid,
committed the foul crime of adultery.

To the twelfth article of the said libel, this deponent says, that some time in or about the month
of Febuary last, he attended the aforesaid Lord
Ancram and Lady Belmore from their said house
in the neighbourhood of Edinburgh, to a house
situate in Queen-street, Edgware-road. That on
the road from Edinburgh to London, they assumed
the names of Mr. and Mrs. Anderson, passed for
husband and wife, and lay at the different inns on
the road in one and the same bed.

That ever since their arrival in Queen street
aforesaid, they the said right honourable William
Kerr, commonly called the Earl of Ancram, and the
said right honourable Henrietta Viscountess Belmore,

more, have lived and cohabited together as man and wife, and laid in one and the fame bed, and are called aud known in Queen-ftreet, and the neighbourhood thereof, by the names of Mr. and Mrs. Anderfon, and they ftill continue fo to live and cohabit together in Queen-ftreet aforefaid; and further to this article he cannot depofe.

To the thirteenth article of this allegation, the deponent fays, that during the laft eleven months, the articulate right honourable Henrietta Vifcountefs Belmore hath not been in Ireland, or had, as this deponent doth verily and in his confcience believe, any intercourfe or connection with the articulate right honourable Armar Lowry Corry, Vifcount Belmore, the party in this caufe. And he further fays, that when he left the faid Lady Belmore's fervice on the fecond of laft month, fhe was then with child, and expected foon to lie in; and further to this article he cannot fay.

To the fourteenth article of the faid libel, this deponent fays, that the faid right honourable Vifcountefs Belmore, previous to her elopement with the aforefaid right honourable William Kerr, commonly called Earl of Ancram, and fince her return to England as aforefaid, was and is of the parifh of St. Mary-le-bonne, in the county of Middlefex, and diocefe of London, and, as this deponent believes, was and is fubject to the jurifdiction of this court: and further he cannot fay.

FRANCOIS LE DUC.

MAY 12, 1792.

JOHN POOLE, valet and butler to Lord Belmore, aged thirty-two years and upwards, produced and fworn.

TO the thirteenth article of the faid libel, this deponent fays, that he hath lived in the fervice of the faid Lord Belmore, for upwards of eight years, and for the laft five years it has been part of his duty to be attending on his mafter on his travels, and at all other times, that he can take upon himfelf pofitively to fwear that, excepting for only ten days in the month of March laft, when he was by his faid mafter fent to England, and alfo for two days in the month of February laft, that he hath been conftantly and daily attending on the faid Lord Belmore, ever fince the 4th day of June laft; and that fince the 4th day of June the faid right honourable Armar Lowry Corry, Vifcount Belmore, has lived and refided altogether at Caftle Coole, and other places in the kingdom of Ireland; and that he hath never (unlefs in the aforefaid ten days) fince the 4th of June laft, been out of the faid kingdom, or had any intercourfe or connection with the articulate right honourable Henrietta Vifcountefs Belmore, his wife, who hath not, to this deponent's knowledge, or belief, been in Ireland during the faid time.

JOHN POOLE.

MAY 12, 1792.

FELIX MAGUIRE, who lived in the fervice of Lord Belmore, for about five years, proved to the fame effect as his fellow-fervant John Poole, viz that during the time he lived with his faid mafter, he had no connection whatever with his faid incontinent wife.

JAMES

MAY 12, 1792.

JAMES CORRY NICHOLSON, Efq. of the Middle Temple, proved the ferving of Lady Belmore with a citation from the court, at Gilmeriton, about five miles from Edinburgh, with whom he left a copy of the original citation.

The

Ingram Content Group UK Ltd.
Milton Keynes UK
UKHW031907160323
418676UK00009B/351